Table of Contents

1. BOOK DESCRIPTION

Do you love puppies? Would love to a have a decent pup with good behaviors?

You have landed to the right guide book, all the training guidelines and lessons are properly written to help you ease your puppy training sessions.

Although it might be tedious but bear in mind that there is nothing like a smooth mountain, persistent and patience are all needed.

This book brings together different puppy training methods and techniques which are proven to work best for your pup. It also provides best and successful methods, with easy-to-follow ways to assist a pup in developing clean living habits and a feeling of security in his new environment.

As a puppy owner, **you will learn** helpful tips such as:
- Importance of having a puppy
- What you need before you start

- Health Check
- Understanding How the Puppies mind works
- Different kind of breeds
- First commands, threats, and feeding
- Bedtime routines and much more

2. KNOW AND EXAMINE YOUR PUPPY
2.1. What you need before you start

Training a puppy is hard work; you should always do your research before getting a puppy. Make sure everyone in the house is aware of what the puppy is and is not allowed to do.

Finding a local professional trainer with good reviews is a good place to start if this is your first puppy. Having a professional there will help you best cope with your little fur ball and learn the steps to having a well behaved, calm dog who's always under control.

2.2. Health check

You know how you couldn't sleep when you're not feeling well? It's the same for puppies, too.

The first thing that you have to keep in mind is that **a puppy's health should be in tip-top shape** because if not, you really would not be able to feed him well and help him to sleep. The pointers below will help you understand whether or not your puppy's health is in check:

- **Eyes** - Let's start with the eyes. Remember that a healthy puppy has eyes that are shiny and clear, without any discharge, or the slightest form of cloudiness.
- **Ears** - Another easy way of seeing whether or not a puppy is healthy is by checking his ears. A puppy's ears have to look and smell clean, and there should not be any redness or inflammation outside or inside the ears. You'll know that a puppy is suffering from an infection if his ears are malodorous and if you see some yellow or brown discharge.

- **Nose** - When a puppy's nose is slightly moist, it means that he is healthy, and sweating in a good way. However, you should take note that his nose does not have to be wet, and there has to be no form of discharge there. N.B.: Persistent sniffing and sneezing are big signs that a puppy is not in good shape.

- **Coat and Skin** – In addition, you have to check if the puppy's coat is actually soft, and it also has to be shiny. Check if there are any flakes around. This is a sign that he might be infected with something, or that his coat has been irritated by harsh sunlight.

- **Other things** you could check regarding skin are sores, bumps, redness, patches, and missing hair. The coat and skin also should not smell pungent. Fleas and ticks may also be around, so always make sure to check for them.

- **Abdomen** - It is okay to feel the puppy's ribs, but make sure that the ribs do not poke out. Otherwise, it is a sign that the puppy is malnourished. A round tummy is also good, but it should never be swollen, and your dog also should not be potbellied.

- **Rear End** - Of course, you also have to check your puppy's butt. Make sure it is clean, and that it's free from any fecal matter or debris of any sort.

- **Behavior** - And finally, a puppy's behavior also comes into play. It is normal for a puppy to be sleepy, but never lethargic. Puppies are naturally playful, and friendly to their littermates. In case they begin to isolate themselves, it means they may not be feeling well, and that they're lonely. And, a healthy puppy is one who's excited to eat, not one who does not even mind food on his bowl.

2.3. First veterinary exam

It's also important that you **bring your puppy to the vet** for his first general veterinary exam. This is done to help determine the health condition of your lovely pet, and if he's experiencing any illnesses and the like. While there, you can expect the vet to:

- **Check your puppy's ears** to see if they look and smell right and that he's not suffering from infections of any kind.
- **Check the puppy's temperature**, which normally ranges from 100 to 125 F. Breathing and pulse rate will be checked, too.
- **Check your puppy's weight**. He'll know if your puppy is normal, underweight, or overweight.
- **Listen for any abnormalities** in the heart and lungs, as well as feel organs, and check for palpitations.
- **Check the puppy's mouth** and see if teeth and gums are in normal condition.
- **Check eyes**, skin, nose, and anal region to see if there are signs of parasites or diseases.
- **Check the puppy's genitals**. For females, he'll check for signs of infection or discharge. For males, he'll check if both testicles are present.

If you see that your puppy is experiencing things that you are meant to be aware of, take that as a sign that it's time to bring him to the vet. Signs that your puppy needs immediate care are listed below:

- Any form of eye injury. Nothing is considered "mild" when it comes to that.
- Hives, swelling, and any other allergic reactions, especially those in the belly.
- Signs of pain, such as loss of appetite, restlessness, lethargy, increased body temperature, labored breathing and panting.
- Respiratory problems, such as trouble breathing, or chronic coughing.

- Animal bites, wounds, lacerations, especially those that are open.
- Suspected poisoning, such as indigestion of human medication, snail or rodent bait, and antifreeze.
- Diarrhea or vomiting, especially if he experiences it more than twice or thrice in an hour.
- Any form of collapse, fainting, or seizure.

Remember that prevention is always better than cure, and this way, you'll be able to focus on improving his sleeping habits, and his health, in general!

Keep all household cleaners and chemicals put away in an area your puppy can't get to, including your garage. There are many plants that are toxic to dogs. The parts that are toxic on the plant can be the leaves, roots, or bulbs. If your puppy is sick and you, or your vet, can't figure out why? Suggest the possibility of ingestion of a toxic plant. Be careful using herbicides, pesticides, and insecticides. Your puppy could lick a leaf or chew on a stick that was sprayed with one of these and become seriously ill.

Be sure to get copies of your puppy's health record when you pick him up from the breeder, shelter, or whoever you get him from. Most vets will want to see it because it may contain some information someday that may save your puppy's life. If you own a large breed puppy, wait until your vet gives the "okay" before you begin jogging with him and don't allow him to slip on slippery floors. This helps with proper hip development.

For vaccinations, give each shot at two-week intervals. For example, if you give your puppy his DHPP, wait two weeks to give him another shot. The same goes for worming medications. This will help lower the stress to your puppy's system and to know which shot or medication caused your puppy to have a reaction.

If you buy a purebred puppy, be sure his dew claws have been removed. These are the claws that are on the inside of the leg, back or front. It can be very painful for a puppy to catch his dew claw on something and have it ripped out.

Get to know your puppy and his habits. It will be easier to notice if he's sick or injured in any way. Give your puppy vaccinations yourself. Many pet supply catalogs offer vaccines and tell you exactly what to give and where to give it. Talk to your vet about which brands he recommends and questions you may have. Giving vaccinations yourself can save you a considerable amount of money. The more to spend on puppy toys!

If a puppy is ill or injured, he may bite. Keep this in mind if your puppy bites for no apparent reason. If your puppy eats feces, be sure your feeding quality food and he doesn't have worms. If those checkouts, just keep your yard clean. He can't eat what's not there! If you have a hard time giving your puppy pills, try storing them in or near his puppy food. The pills will probably absorb the smell of the puppy food making them easier to give your puppy.

Does your puppy scoot around the floor in a sitting position? He probably needs to have his anal sacs emptied. Do this yourself by gently, but firmly, squeezing on either side of the anus. Have plenty of paper towels handy. It's a dirty job, so it is highly recommended having your vet do it. If your puppy looks or acts seriously ill or injured, call your vet.

Never allow your puppy to stick his head out the window when you're driving down the road. All sorts of debris can get into his eyes. It's safest to leave the window down a few inches and let him feel the air against his face from inside the car.

Never leave your puppy inside a vehicle when it's hot out. It only takes a few minutes for your puppy to die from the heat. Leave your puppy home where he will be cool and comfortable, and alive.

Seriously consider spaying or neutering your puppy within his first year. There are many advantages to this, including behavioral and medical. In females, mammary cancer, which is one of the top cancers in females not spayed, is nearly eliminated.

Uterine cancer, uterine infections, and ovarian cancer are also nearly eliminated in spayed females. Spayed females also have no desire to mate; therefore they won't be tempted to wander in search of a mate. By neutering your male puppy, you eliminate the risk of prostate problems, rectal tumors, and testicular cancer. He will also be less likely to roam since he'll have no desire to mate. Neutering can also make him less aggressive toward other male dogs. And the biggest point of spaying and neutering is that you won't have any unexpected or unwanted puppies.

Here are some different ways to exercise your puppy: walking on lead, free running in an open field, playing fetch, running up and down the stairs, and playing with a plastic ball that can be batted around, but not picked up or gripped in the mouth.

3. KNOW YOUR BREED
3.1. Understanding how the puppy's mind works

It is important for you to bond with your puppy and know what it wants from you or to do. Massaging and grooming your puppy is an excellent way to bond with him. Start with his head then go to his ears, neck, shoulders, front legs, back, sides, and hips. You'll notice him starting to nod off and close his eyes when you start. I've actually seen a few puppies fall over they were so relaxed!

When your puppy bows down (front legs parallel to the ground, hind legs perpendicular to the ground), he's telling you he wants to play. Give him a command, and when he does it, play with him. Keep your puppy under control at all times for his safety and others'. This means keeping him on a leash when outside.

Never take your puppy for a walk down the street without him being leashed. Someday, something may scare him or invite him to chase and he may get hit by a car. Sure you may want to show off how well your puppy heels or how intelligent your puppy is, but the consequences aren't worth it.

Leave the door to your puppy's crate open when he's not in it. Most puppies will view the crate as their den and go in there on their own when they're tired or just need a break from everything.

3.2. What to know about breeds

Purebred - A purebred puppy is one whose parents are both of the same recognized breeds — for example, both parents are Collies or both parents are Dalmatians.

Registered - A registered puppy is one that's purebred and has a record of his birth and his parents' births kept by an organization specializing in registering dogs. For example, both parents are registered German Shepherds and the litter has been registered with the appropriate kennel club or breed club, the puppies are considered registered.

Pedigreed - A pedigree is a record of a puppy's ancestors, usually written as a family tree. Some breeders furnish a pedigree of their own. A certified pedigree can also be ordered from the kennel or breed club with which the puppy is registered. A pedigreed puppy is one for which such an ancestry record has been kept.

Mixed Breed - A mixed-breed puppy is one whose parents are from more than one recognized breed or from undetermined parentage. For example, his father might be a Labrador Retriever and his mother an Irish Setter, or one or both of his parents themselves might be mixed breeds. Many times no one has any idea what a dog's ancestors were because as far back as anyone can remember, they were mixed breeds. Mixed-breed dogs are sometimes called mongrels or mutts.

Crossbred - A crossbred puppy is one whose parents are of two or more different breeds, but their mating was planned deliberately by professional breeders to produce a new breed.

Inbred or Line bred - Inbred or line bred puppies are those whose parents are of the same breed and closely related by family kinship. Experienced dog breeders mate such dogs to reinforce particular inherited traits.

3.3. Considerations between mixed breeds and pure breeds

For a willing puppy owner, it is important to consider the following facts on mixed breeds and purebred puppies.

Mixed Breeds

A mixed-breed puppy or his parents are not of the same breed. You may not be able to find out what breed or mixture of breeds his parents are. If he's a puppy, you may have to guess what he will look like as an adult, how large he will get, and what characteristics he may have inherited from his parents. A cute, cuddly little puppy of eight weeks might turn out to weigh 10 pounds or 100 pounds.

Mixed breeds generally seem to have fewer of the inherited health complications that are common in certain pure breeds. These health complications include deafness, early cancer, and hip dysplasia. Mixed breeds probably have fewer inherited health complications because both parents are not the same breed and are less apt to carry the matching problem genes.

How Big Will that Mixed-Breed Puppy Get?

One way to get an idea of whether a puppy will grow up into a large or small dog is to look at his bone structure, especially in his legs and paws. A puppy with a large bone structure and heavy legs and paws will most likely grow up to be much larger and heavier than one of the same age with fine bones and small legs and paws. Some breeds that have a fine bone structure, however, grow up to be very tall; the Greyhound is an example.

Pure Breeds

Purebred dogs were bred by people to have specific characteristics of the structure, hair coat, color, size, abilities, and temperament.

The genetic makeup of the pure breed is easily changed by selective breeding. By choosing particular physical and character traits, and then breeding dogs that have those traits, people have developed purebred dogs that can perform amazing roles.

Dogs have been specially bred to hunt game, track prisoners, guard and defend property and people, herd cattle and sheep, work with police, run races, sniff for drugs and other illegal items, dig out badgers, seek out rats, provide companionship, and more.

3.4. When to begin training?

Puppy training is an activity that has an immense contribution to a dog's life in terms of behavior and response.

Puppy training is a very important aspect in the growth and development of a dog. This is due to the fact that it plays a great role in determining the manner in which the puppy will behave once it is a fully grown dog. It is, therefore, important to introduce your puppy to such training at a very young age, probably at the tenth week.

4. GETTING STARTED
4.1. First day at home

Be sure to puppy proof your home before you bring your puppy home.

The easiest way to do this is to lie on the floor in each room and scan the area from the floor to about 2-3 feet up.

Hide electric cords, put up plants and breakables, put away any rodent poisons or traps and cleaners, and anything else within your puppy's reach that you don't want to be eaten, destroyed, or harm your puppy.

4.2. First commands, threats, and feeding

Be consistent when training your puppy or he will get confused as to when or if to listen.
If you tell him to sit, make him sit.
If you tell him to stay, make him stay.
If you don't want him on the couch, never let him on the couch.

If you don't want him jumping on you, don't let him jump up.

You have to do it when it needs to be done, or you'll pay the price tenfold! <u>Basic commands are the foundation of obedience training</u>.
You could sign your puppy up for professional obedience training lessons, but you may want to attempt teaching the commands on your own first. If your puppy catches on quickly, then you could save some money by at least teaching the basic skills on your own.

Following are effective strategies for teaching all of the basic commands. **Remember to use the same word** every time you work on a command. Your dog will learn what you want them to do according to that exact sound, so the terms cannot be switched up. Stay consistent!

"Come"

This is typically the first command you will teach your puppy. You can teach it simultaneously with **"sit"** and **"stay."** You are essentially telling your puppy to come to you. The key is to teach your puppy that coming to you is a pleasant experience. You never call your puppy to you and then put them on a leash, throw them right into the crate, or otherwise send a signal of punishment.

Rather, call them to you and give them a small treat for a prompt response. Love on them. Slip them a small treat. Start by giving treats just for coming when called, and then start giving them only when they come and sit as commanded. Finally, wean out the treats, so they get used to coming just for a pat on the head and a bit of attention.
Work with this command throughout your puppy's life. By adulthood, they should be well trained to come to you on command.

"Sit"

You can use small treats as well as praise and love to get your puppy to come to you and sit on command. Your goal should be to train them to sit and stay, so work with these two commands together. Start by gently pushing down on the backside of the puppy while giving this command. You should only have to do this a couple times before they catch on to what **"sit"** means.

After that, command them to sit after getting their attention and give them a small treat. Start by rewarding just the sit. You can then start rewarding only when they sit and stay for a couple seconds. Start this training at home without any distractions. With time you can practice around other people, in public places, and with other distractions that will make the puppy want to get up and run.

Eventually, you want your puppy to come to you, sit down, and stay put. A well-trained puppy will eventually grow into a well-trained adult dog able to stay by its owner's side even when there are serious distractions, such as a bird playing in a puddle nearby. That level of training takes time, so be patient.

"Shake"
 This is probably the easiest trick to teach your puppy. Have your puppy sit in front of you. Tell him "shake" and grab his front paw and give it a gentle shake. Then give him a treat. Do this a couple times. After the fifth or sixth time, tell him "shake" and just put your hand in front of him and see if he'll offer his paw. If he does, really praise him and give him a treat. If not, grab his paw and keep repeating until he'll offer his paw on his own.

4.3. Potty training

It is time to potty train your puppy by use Clicker training. This method is based on the popular **"clicker training"**. Instead of using the clicker for every aspect of training, you'll be using it for potty training only, thereby increasing its effectiveness. If you don't have a clicker, visit your nearest pet store.

You can use this method whether you have a puppy or dog, work all day or are at home, or if you've already started a different potty training method and it hasn't worked. Simply **throw out the other ideas you've had** about potty training and start fresh. This method is so easy to teach and most puppies and dogs will catch on extremely quickly.

Keep in mind though that your puppy will need to have **a good diet and a strict schedule**. No puppy will become potty trained if he is fed "less than quality" food and if he's fed whenever. You need to be completely dedicated, no matter how tired you are! Remember, a puppy learns only what he has been taught. Your puppy's good behavior, or lack of, reflects directly on you!

Before you begin with this method, you need to set your puppy up for success. Since your puppy is young, chances are he simply can't hold it for more than a few hours at a time. It would be very cruel of us to expect him to hold it all day so be prepared to clean up messes until he's around 3-5 months of age. To help control where he messes in the house you will need to set up a room or a large crate. These will be large enough for him to have areas to play, sleep, and mess. If we don't give him room to do these things he will probably develop the nasty habit of messing where he sleeps. This is a very difficult habit to break so let's prevent it from the very beginning. If you use a room or exercise pen, it will work well if you use a crate for him to sleep in. This will prepare him for when he's older and you want to crate him when you leave.

When you set up the area he will use when alone, be sure he has something comfortable to sleep on, and the material you want him to normally mess on outside. If you want him to always go on the grass, place a piece of sod in his area. One piece should last nearly a week if you just clean up the poop. You want to leave the urine smell in the sod since this will attract your puppy back to the sod. If you prefer he always go on the cement outside, get a thin slab of cement for his area. Again, just clean off the poop and every few days rinse the slab with plain water.

Now we're ready to begin! If you haven't brought your puppy home yet plan on starting this from the second, you pick him up.

If you already have your puppy, start this when you'll have a few full days to work on it. First, we need to associate the clicker with something very good. This is one of the few times you'll hear me say to use treats when training, but there is no better reward for a puppy than a tasty treat!

And what behavior other than going to the bathroom outside deserves something this good? Grab your puppy, the clicker, and a few treats you know your puppy likes. It will be advisable to do this outside on the surface you want him to use, at his designated potty spot, since you'll always be clicking and treating his behavior outside.

All you need to do now is click a few times then give him a treat. Choose how many times you'll click the clicker, so he knows what he's doing well every time. Once or twice should suffice. Be sure to only give him a small piece of the treat. Don't give him a whole mouthful. Continue to click and treat every few minutes. Once he hears the clicks and looks to you for a treat you know, he's caught on. Now we wait until he goes to the bathroom. As soon as he starts to pee or poop click the clicker, however, many times you've decided on. When he's finished, give him a treat and really praise him. Put your clicker away until the next time you take him out to the bathroom. Repeat this every time he goes.

Now you're probably wondering how to handle it when he goes in the house. Well, you do nothing but clean it up.

Provided you click and treat every time he goes to the bathroom outside he will catch on that good things happen when he goes outside, but nothing happens when he goes in the house. Before long, he'll want to go outside all the time to go to the bathroom and get a treat.

By using a few days to get him used to his spot outside on the surface you've chosen, chances are he'll go on that same surface in the house. If he doesn't, try making his indoor mess area a little bigger or placing a small chunk of sod where he's previously gone pee on top of his indoor sod. Before long, you should have a puppy that willingly holds it until he can get outside.

NOTE: Don't expect too much from a puppy under 12-16 weeks old or a small breed puppy, though. Young and very small puppies just aren't physically capable of holding it that long.

This should only be started after at least two weeks of no accidents in the house and your pup letting you know consistently that he needs to go out. We can now assume that your puppy understands that he is expected to go to the bathroom outside and that he'll let you know it, so it should be safe to begin! Start this on a weekend morning or anytime you'll have a few days to dedicate to this.

Take him out as you normally would in the morning. Click and treat as normal for this time. The next time you take him out, don't click but give a treat. Couple this with plenty of praise. Take him back in and wait until the next time he needs to go out. Click and treat for this one. Do the click and treat for every other bathroom break for the rest of the day. If he seems okay with everything and is still going to the door to be let out, with no accidents in the house, we can move on to the next day. If he backslides even one time with either not letting you know he needs to go out or going to the bathroom in the house, go back to click and treating every time. He obviously isn't ready.

Give him a few more days and try again. If everything went smoothly your first day, click and treat every third bathroom break. Continue this for a few days and if all is well, try eliminating the click and treat altogether for one day. If he has accidents in the house go back a step. If all goes well, forget the click and treat for a few days and monitor his behavior. If he seems okay with the new arrangement, pat yourself on the back! You now have a potty trained puppy!

If your puppy makes a mistake in the house, go back one step and continue working on that particular step for a few days. Some puppies may catch on to this right away and others may take weeks or even months. Keep in mind that you shouldn't use the clicker for any other training. You don't want to confuse him, do you?

You can alter this method to fit your needs for other potty training. If you want to train your pup to mess in a litter box, simply click every time he goes in it. Follow the same guidelines, with the exception of teaching him how to let you know he needs to go out. Or if you have a doggy door, you can teach this method with much quicker results. Set your pup's pen up in front of the doggy door when you're gone and he'll be potty trained in no time! First, you must teach him to go out the doggy door. This is a matter of simply coaxing him through it, while you hold it open, to get his dinner. Do this a few times until he seems okay with it. Then close the door and have someone coax him through to the other side. This shouldn't take much more than a few times. When teaching with the use of a doggy door keep in mind that you'll still need to go out with him to click and treat. Let him go out the doggy door and once he's through you simply go out behind out.

Consult your vet if you feel your puppy is going way too much or not enough because some potty training problems are caused by the puppy or dog being sick. Don't expect too much from your puppy either. He's a puppy and will do what comes naturally or what was unintentionally taught to him. It's your job to teach him what is and isn't acceptable behavior. Don't slack off because you feel your puppy is stupid and incapable of learning or because you've just had it with trying to teach him to go outside for three weeks and he's still messing in the house.

All puppies can and will learn if given the proper instruction and time to learn. So get ready to begin properly potty training your puppy! Before we begin, take note of these potty training do's and don'ts.

4.4. Potty Training Do's

- Take your puppy out when he wakes up, after eating and drinking, when you first get home, and after play sessions.

- Take him outside through the same door.

- Take him to the same spot.

- Bring him back in through the same door.

- Take your puppy out on a leash.

- Clean up messes inside with a solution of half vinegar and half water.

- Choose a phrase as his "bathroom" signal and use it as soon as you get him to his spot.

- Leave a few stools at his bathroom area.

- Rush your puppy outside if he starts to mess in the house.
- Keep him on a set schedule for feeding, walking, etc.

4.5. Potty Training Don'ts

- Don't rub your puppy's nose in his mess.

- Don't leave him in his crate for longer periods than he can handle.

- Don't scold him for making a mess in the house.

- Don't hit your puppy for messing in the house.

- Don't play with him before he goes to the bathroom.

- Don't let him have the run of the house before he's fully trustworthy.

- Don't scold your puppy if he starts to mess in the house.

- Don't use newspaper when potty training. They're messy and confuse your pup.

- Don't use different doors to take him outside and back in.

- Don't ignore your puppy's need to go out no matter how tired you are.

4.6. The puppy doorbell

Once your puppy has had no accidents in the house for at least 2 weeks, **it's time to start teaching** him to let you know when he needs to go out. After teaching him how to let you know he needs to go out, it's time to start eliminating the clicker and treats.

Everyone wants their puppy to notify them when he needs to go out. You'll have to decide how you want your puppy to let you know. Most people don't want their puppies jumping on the door or scratching at the door since this only create damaged doors. The best method to avoid such damages is to **use the puppy door bell**. You simply hang a bell from your door knob; mount it on the wall at your puppy's level. Or you can use another method of teaching your puppy to bark when he needs to go out. However, this method can be difficult to teach since many puppies won't bark until they're older, and some breeds just aren't inclined to bark.

Before you install the doorbell, your puppy needs to know that messing is supposedly done outside only. Your puppy should be fully trustworthy when you're home with him in the house. It works best at this time because your puppy knows he should go outside, but he just doesn't know how to get out. And at this time, he should be old enough to hold it for longer periods, allowing you to take him out at certain times without having to clean up any messes in the house.

Once you've got your bell in place, you'll need to **show your puppy the bell**. Encourage him to sniff it or lick it. If he happens to make it sound off open the door and take him out. If he doesn't make it sound off, you can do it, then open the door and take him out. It also advisable to have your puppy leashed when you practice with the bell, so you have control of him when you take him out. Of course, every time he does something good be sure to praise him; whether he touches the bell, makes it sound off, looks at the door after making noise, anything. Be most lavish with your praise if he rings the bell then looks to the door.

Have him ring the bell every time before you go out and very soon he should catch on that ringing the bell opens the door which allows him to go to the bathroom. Be very vigilant about this and before too long you will hear the bell when you're watching television. This is the time when you really praise and let him know how he is. **Immediately take him outside** to his spot.

4.7. Crate or pen training

Crate training is one of the most popular forms of puppy training. You purchase a crate of suitable size for your puppy from a pet store and use it to limit the puppy's access to your home. You never want to turn an untrained puppy loose in your home, even for short periods of time.

The puppy does not yet know how to behave in your home and will undoubtedly chew a hole in your couch cushion, tear down the curtains, or scratch a hole in your carpet trying to dig out from under a door.

Crate training confines the puppy when they cannot be directly supervised. If you will be out of the home most of the day to work, it is a good idea to get the puppy used to the crate right away. Just make sure they are never left in the cage so long that they have to potty in the crate.

You can use the crate to help the puppy learn to hold their bladder during potty training, but they should never be left more than four or five hours at a stretch when you first start this training.

The basic premise of **crate training is simple**. When you need to keep the puppy safe from danger and out of trouble, you put them in the crate. You bring them out for feedings and potty breaks, and of course, to play with them and love them. Then they go back into the crate. This continues until they are completely potty trained and can be trusted in your home without direct supervision.

The Secret to Crate Training

Your puppy must see their crate as their **safe place**; **their bed**; **their comfy place** to retire. If they are left in the crate for long periods of time and/or neglected of your love and attention, they will see their crate as a place of punishment. They will fight you every time you try to put them in that crate. They will whine, cry and howl every time they are locked in there.

Crate training will be an option for many of the training strategies presented throughout this book. When considering this option, always keep in mind this secret to crate training. Your training will not be effective if your pup decides the crate is punishment, rather than their safe haven.

When used correctly, **your puppy will love going in his crate** even after he has been turned free to roam the home. They will go to this bed when they are tired, when they want to hide from unusual activity, or just when they want to hide a bone.

4.8. Stop from nipping or biting

Many puppies go through a stage of biting everything from your hand to your stocking feet. As soon as biting begins it should be nipped in the bud, so to speak.

Your puppy doesn't really intend to hurt you when they bite; they explore much of the world with their mouths. When your puppy mouths you pay close attention. When the bite gets too hard or starts to hurt be sure to let out a loud sound. Yelps and "**Ouch**" do well. The startle of volume will make him stop biting. When he releases walk away for a short period of time say 10-20 seconds then resume playing. It takes time, but your puppy will catch on and learn that biting is something he shouldn't do.

Natural Consequences

Allowing your puppy to experience the natural consequences of their feisty behavior is perhaps the most efficient way to teach them to tame this behavior. Naturally, puppies learn not to bite by playing with their parents and litter mates. When they get too rough and hurt each other, they will naturally put one another in place. They learn as they grow **to treat one another with respect** and to play in a gentle, safe manner.

If you have puppies around the same age, then you can simply allow them to play together to start the process of eliminating biting during play. If you have only one puppy, then finding other dogs for them to play with is vital. Just make sure those other dogs are not overly aggressive, as that will teach your puppy to be rougher, rather than gentler.

The Right Response

You have to make sure everyone with access to your puppy responds to a bite or nip in the same manner. You do not want to yell at them, strike them, or throw them into their crate. Even if they bite kind of hard and it hurts, you have to respond with a firm, "**No**." You can also put them down if they are on your lap, or get up if you are on the floor. Removing yourself from contact with the puppy shows them that the biting and nipping is not acceptable. Importantly, you have to go back and show a bit of love to your puppy, so they know you are not mad at them. It is the behavior you are trying to correct, so your puppy must know you still love them.

Consistency Is Key

You have to respond immediately and in the same manner, every time you see an unacceptable behavior in your puppy. A playful puppy will learn rather quickly that biting a playmate instantly ends the play session. If you can give them active play time with other dogs or puppies as well, they will learn even faster.

4.9. Play nice with other dogs

There are a variety of social problems that can develop if a puppy is not properly socialized early in life. **Some puppies may become fearful** of other dogs, which leads to dog aggression. Other dogs may become overly excited when they do come in contact with other dogs. Many dogs will not know how to properly play with other dogs, so they may struggle to make friends or may anger other dogs as they get older.

The best thing you can do is start exposing your puppy to other dogs of all ages and sizes, as well as humans. Do this as soon as your puppy has received all of their shots and is protected from illnesses other dogs may pass on to them. It is often advised that a puppy is well socialized before they turn five or six months old, so it is never too early to start.

Allow your puppy to interact with other dogs in your home. Just make sure it is supervised and the new puppy is not being treated aggressively, as that passes on aggressive behavior.
Allow them to interact with dogs owned by your friends and relatives. Take them to the dog park. Do not turn them off of the leash until you are confident they can interact with other dogs properly. Try to **keep them with dogs their own size** and age at first. Take them out for walks in a variety of locations. Get them used to seeing other dogs and being in crowds without becoming scared or overly excited.

It is also important to other dogs to walk through your backyard while your puppy is young. This helps them accept the fact that this territory of theirs may occasionally be used by other dogs and that it is okay.

5. BEDTIME ROUTINES

As a puppy owner, it is important to ensure that the puppy has a good and adequate sleep. Just like humans, you could not expect puppies to just go to sleep even if their surroundings are not in a proper condition. The first thing you have to keep in mind is that it is **important to provide them with a clean environment**. This can be achieved by following the following steps:

Provide Them with a Space All Their Own
Puppies need to feel safe and secure in their environment. That is why you have to give them a space in the house that they could consider their own den. It could either be their own room or maybe even place their bed in your bedroom, so they would know that you are around and they are safe.

Keep boundaries from other pets
Sometimes, puppies do not mix well with the other pets you have at home, especially if they're of the other kinds, such as cats. You have to keep in mind that you cannot expect them to just mingle with one another right away. They have to be familiarized with each other's scents first. It is a way of helping them get to know each other.

The sense of ownership is important for pets, too If you get a new puppy and let him stay in the bed that's owned by other pets, your other pets may harbor ill feelings towards you and that is not something you want to happen. Try not to make the pets fight on the get-go. Fighting makes them stressed and does not make it easy for them to sleep.

The Right Bed
Puppies also like sleeping on comfortable beds. Sometimes, the kind of bed they sleep in would determine whether they'd sleep well or not.

5.1. Different beds suitable for puppies

- **Bolster Beds** - Bolster beds are quite comfortable and most puppies feel at home in one. Bolster beds are like padded beds but provide additional support for the puppies because they could rest their heads at elevated angles.

- **Cedar-Filled Beds** - are also padded beds and could be purchased from most pet stores. The difference between these beds and typical padded beds is the fact that cedar-filled beds are created to mask a pet's odor, especially in confined spaces. However, since the bed is trying to mask your pet's odor, the bed emits the smell of cedar and the bed might be a problem if you are not comfortable with that smell. Dogs may also find the smell a bit annoying, and you'd see them roll around a little too much.

- **Cots** - Cots are lifted slightly above the ground and could be placed outside, so that the puppy could have a place to rest outdoors, too. Cots are also recommended for dogs with thick coats because they provide proper air circulation so the dog would not be in heat.

- **Simple Padded** - are the most common kind of pet beds. They're basically just pillows covered with soft and comfortable materials and are also stuffed, mostly with cotton. They're also the most affordable pet beds, making them a favorite of many pet owners.

- Orthopedic Beds - Orthopedic beds are mainly used for old, arthritic dogs. But, if your puppy is suffering from hip dysplasia, or has recently survived an accident, orthopedic beds may help them sleep, too. Orthopedic beds are designed in such a way that the dog's body would not touch the ground so his back would not hurt. They also decrease the amount of cold that a dog feels because of extra padding. This way, his condition would not worsen, and his joints would start recuperating.

- Corner Bed - Corner beds are perfect for puppies, and small dog breeds, as well as for houses that are not very spacious because they're meant to fit in the corner of a room.

- Cave Bed - Cave beds give some puppies a sense of security because they know they could hide in them. The beds are characterized by having a hood, which makes for easy snuggling.

- Heated and Cooled Beds - are special kinds of beds that are meant for puppies who are experiencing medical problems. They could either be cooled or heated, depending on the weather so that the puppy could easily adjust and sleep.

- Crates - Crates give the puppy a den-like experience and preferred by most puppy owners. Crates are very crucial in training the puppy how to keep the house in order and not wandering all over the house.

5.2. Playpens

While training your puppy, you can also make use of playpens just to acclimatize your puppy to his new space. Playpens are essential for:

- Helping the puppy separate his thoughts from playtime and sleeping.
- Helping the puppy get to know other pets, without the risk of having them fight because they're in one small area alone.
- Keeping the puppy safe, especially if you're trying to fix some things in the house.

- Helping him enjoy the outdoors, without being at risk of being attacked, or meeting accidents.

5.3. Feeding time

A puppy will also sleep better if you feed him at the right time. This is around 3 to 5 hours before he sleeps.

You can **feed him 2 to 3 hours before he sleeps** but make sure it's nothing too heavy. This is because the puppy's bladder becomes full, and of course, that is a sign that they'll probably wake up to pee or defecate in the middle of the night, which can be inconvenient.

5.4. Bring his security items with you

With time, you'll realize that your puppy has certain items that make him feel secure. Usually, it's in the form of a blanket. If you're traveling or going somewhere for the night, and you're bringing your puppy with you, make sure **to bring his security items**, too. This will make it easy for him to sleep. It could also be done when you're bringing him to the vet, and if he has to stay there overnight.

5.5. Simple rules

In helping your puppy sleep, there are certain things that you have to do. Follow the steps below and you'll surely be able to help your puppy go to bed at the right time and help you catch up on sleep, too!

Fix his bed.
The first thing you have to do is make sure your puppy's bed is made-up. This way, once you bring him inside the room, he'll know that it'll be okay for him to go to sleep and that the day is over.

Go potty!
As mentioned in an earlier chapter, it's always good to bring your puppy to his potty area shortly before going to bed. This way, he would be able to associate this action to the fact that he should do his dirty now, so both of you could go to bed later.

Establish a routine.
You know how you have some kind of routine before going to bed? You can do that for your puppy, too. For example, every

night before going to bed, go and give your dog a lukewarm bath or just wash his body with lukewarm cloth. Then, play with him a bit just until he gets tired and then go and give him his blanket or his favorite pillow. This has a lot to do with observation, you see. You'd often notice your being comfortable once his close to a certain toy or certain part of his bed at bed- time. Give him that. Or, you might see him kneading or hugging his bed, or his toys at this time - allow him. This way, he'd know he's safe, and there would be some sense of security. This would then make it easier for him to sleep. When puppies need sleep, they sleep. You may be playing with your puppy one second and the next he's sound asleep. This is what puppies do!

6. COMMON BEHAVIOR ISSUES
6.1. Incessant, whining and howling

There are few things more exhausting than a puppy insistent on howling, whining and barking through the night. You can expect some agitation when you first start crate training a puppy, but **you have to work** with the whining and barking immediately, so you do not reinforce that behavior.

For instance, if you let the puppy out of the crate just to shut them up, you can guarantee they will whine and bark even louder next time. You have reinforced that behavior **by sending the message** that whining and barking brings an exit from the crate.

You first have to ensure that all of the puppy's needs are being met, that they are comfortable in their crate, and that they are not suffering in any manner medically.

You have likely already had the puppy checked out by a vet, so health conditions or internal pain should be ruled out already. Check off the following items just to make sure there is nothing you can do to easily calm your new pup down: **The puppy is being fed adequate amounts of food each day**. The puppy has been let out to potty within the past few hours.

The crate is large enough for the puppy to stand up and turn around comfortably. There are blankets or bedding in the crate to keep the puppy comfortable and warm.

The puppy is not infested with fleas or ticks and has no rashes or skin irritations. The puppy has been exercised and given ample opportunity to burn off energy before bedtime. You have given the puppy something to chew on if they are teething.

If all of these things have been taken care of and your puppy is still whining and barking, then they are more than likely trying to get attention. Puppies love to be cuddled, and they are happiest when in the company of others. They will have to get used to being in their crate. Here are some tips on getting through the first night or two without losing sleep:

Take the puppy out for a walk, play ball, or perform some other type of vigorous exercise just before putting them to bed. Give them a good hour of exercise to burn off their energy.

Put him in the crate at least an hour before you plan to go to bed yourself. This gives him time to give up the whining before you are ready to sleep. Do not feed the puppy right before putting him in the crate. You want him to digest his food and poop before going into the crate.

A new puppy can be like a newborn baby. They may cry the first night or two, but they will get used to going to bed as long as they are well cared for before going down for the night.

6.2. Chewing the house

A teething puppy will chew anything and everything that they can get their little mouths around. If you have a large breed puppy that is growing quickly, you could have a big slobbery mouth chewing on your table legs, bedroom suit, and even your children's toys. As soon as you decide to bring a puppy into your home, you have to bring out the puppy toys to spare your home from becoming one big teething toy.

Ideally, you will already have your puppy under close supervision. Inappropriate chewing and gnawing become just one more thing that you have to watch out for and immediately correct. **Catching the puppy in action and redirecting his efforts** to something more appropriate is the most effective way to send the message that your home is not to be chewed.

Unfortunately, you have to redirect that attention away from the inappropriate chewing repeatedly until your puppy fully gets the message. A puppy only adjust his behavior if he has an alternative that he know is more appropriate and approved by you. This means that **you have to correct and redirect as soon as you notice** he is chewing something and give him an alternative that is acceptable.

7. ONE WEEK PLAN

Here's a sample schedule that you can try to help create a routine for your puppy, and help him learn things with ease:

- Upon waking up, take the puppy to his potty place.
- After peeing and defecating, go for a brisk walk, and go ahead and play with the dog. You can try fetch or any other game that would require your dog to participate. Do this for around 10 minutes.
- Spend another 10 minutes as "quality time" for you and your puppy. Just pet and talk to him, and use this time to check if there is anything wrong with him, such as his coat, his attitude, his eyes, etc.
- Now, it's time for your puppy to eat! Give him fresh puppy chow, and make sure his water is fresh and clean, too.
- Bring the puppy out again to pee or defecate. This is inherent to them, especially after meals.
- If you're going to go to work, your puppy should take a nap. Or, you could play with him, or ask somebody else to do it.
- After the nap, play with the dog again or go out with him for a walk. Just give him time to enjoy his surroundings.
- If you're home, allow your puppy to watch you move around the house.
- Change your puppy's water, feed him, and play with him again. It's good to let him play until he gets tired so it would be easier for him to sleep.
- Now's the time for another "quality time" with your puppy. You could use it for grooming him, talking to him, or letting him watch TV or listen to music with you.
- Finally, before going to bed, bring your puppy to his potty place one more time.

However, it is important to note the following in your schedule:

- Puppies won't be able to sleep unless they've had enough opportunities to play and go to their potty place. Make sure that if you cannot be around with them the whole day, they have a lot of toys, other pets, or people to play with. Just like you, puppies really do not want to get bored, too. Puzzle or chew toys are helpful because they easily keep puppies preoccupied. The key here is that if the puppy was able to utilize his day well, he would not have a hard time sleeping at night— which will also be good for you!
- A comfortable environment. Don't expect puppies to enjoy time with you if your house looks like an entire mess. If you have an indoor puppy, it's always best to make sure that his surroundings are clean, and that there are no awful odors and that you're able to give him the kind of life that he deserves.
- Feed the puppy once or twice a day. There are some puppies who like to eat once every four to five hours, though, especially those from smaller breeds. The important thing is to make sure that your dog is properly fed so he wouldn't wake up hungry, or too full, in the middle of the night. Puppies always need to be fed much more than dogs as they are still growing. Plus, always check your puppy's appetite. There are days when he'd want to eat more, and when there are times that he does not want to eat, maybe you should check if he's experiencing any illnesses or conditions.
- Eliminating is important. While dogs only need to do so at least once every 8 hours, puppies need to be let out more often since their bodies are only adjusting to a routine.
- Say a magic word. It's also good if you could provide your dog with a magic word that would help him realize it's time to sleep. For example bed, sleep, good night, sleep now, etc. It's important to say this every time he goes to bed, so he will associate the act of sleeping with it.

- Time is essential. And of course, make sure that you give your puppy ample amounts of time. Puppies need to feel comforted, and loved, and if you don't have enough time for them, why did you even get them in the first place? When a puppy is loved, he won't feel the need to ask for your attention especially in the middle of the night.

8. CONCLUSION

Puppy training can turn out to be a bit difficult effort, but hard work and persistence pay off. Remember that everything that seems like a simple process can become a tedious routine if not done correctly from the outset. As a novice, you may make avoidable mistakes when training your pup and this may be time-consuming, waste of energy and can be frustrating too. Not to mention that it can be confusing and scary for your little cute puppy.

Training your pup doesn't have to be hard, though. As a matter of fact, this book will make the whole process easy and stress-free, I hope this guide has simplified everything to do with puppy training. Common problems that many people run up against can be avoided just by knowing that they exist. Training your puppy does not have to be tedious and stressful, and with the right approach you will definitely find out it doesn't have to be.

Thank you for reading this book! Good luck in your training!